The Soul of an Indian

The Soul
of an Indian

and Other Writings
from
Ohiyesa
(Charles Alexander Eastman)

Edited and arranged by

KENT NERBURN

THE CLASSIC WISDOM COLLECTION
NEW WORLD LIBRARY
SAN RAFAEL, CALIFORNIA

The Classic Wisdom Collection
Published by New World Library
58 Paul Drive, San Rafael, CA 94903

Cover design: Greg Wittrock
Text design: Nancy Benedict
Typography: TBH/Typecast, Inc.

Library of Congress Cataloging-in-Publication Data

Eastman, Charles Alexander, 1858–1939.
    The soul of an Indian and other writings from Ohiyesa
(Charles Alexander Eastman) / edited and arranged by
Kent Nerburn.
        p. cm. — (The Classic wisdom collection)
    "A reconfiguration of his [i.e., Eastman's] writings, chosen
from a variety of sources, woven together in a way that gives
voice to the spiritual vision that animated all his writing and
speaking."
    ISBN 1-880032-23-6 (acid-free paper) : $12.95
    1. Indians of North America — Religion and mythology.
2. Santee Indians — Religion and mythology.   3. Indians of North
America — Social life and customs.   4. Santee Indians — Social life
and customs.   5. Eastman, Charles Alexander, 1858–1939.
I. Nerburn, Kent, 1946–   II. Series.
E98.R3E148   1993
299'.7 — dc20   93-24678
                                                            CIP

First printing, September 1993
ISBN 1-880032-23-6
Printed in the U.S.A. on acid-free paper

"When you see a new trail, or a footprint you do not know, follow it to the point of knowing."

Uncheedah, the grandmother of Ohiyesa

Contents

Introduction

It is my goal in this book to bring before you the thoughts of one of the most fascinating and overlooked individuals in American history: Ohiyesa, also known by the Anglicized name of Charles Alexander Eastman.

Ohiyesa was, at heart, a poet of the spirit and the bearer of a spiritual vision. To the extent that he dared, and with increasing fervor as he aged, he was a preacher for the native vision of life. It is my considered belief it is his spiritual vision, above all else, that we of our generation need to hear. We hunger for the words and insights of the Native American, and no man spoke with more clarity than Ohiyesa.

Ohiyesa was born in southern Minnesota in the area now called Redwood Falls in the winter of 1858. He was a member of the Santee tribe of the Dakota, or Sioux, nation. When he was four, his people rose up in desperation against the U.S. government, which was systematically starving them by withholding provisions and payment they were owed from the sale of their land.

When their uprising was crushed, more than a thousand men, women, and children were captured and taken away. On the day after Christmas in 1862, thirty-eight of the men were hanged at Mankato, Minnesota, in the greatest mass execution ever performed by the U.S. government. Those who were not killed were taken to stockades and holding camps, where they faced starvation and death during the icy days of the northern winter.

Ohiyesa's father, Many Lightnings, was among those captured.

Ohiyesa, who was among those left behind, was handed over to his uncle to be raised in the traditional Sioux manner. He was taught the ways of the forest and the lessons of his people. He strove to become a hunter and a warrior. Then, one day while he was hunting, he saw an Indian walking toward him in white man's clothes. It was his father, who had survived the internment camps and had returned to claim his son.

During his incarceration, Many Lightnings had seen the power of the European culture and had become convinced that the Indian way of life could not survive within it. He despised what he called "reservation Indians" who gave up their independence and tradition in order to accept a handout from the European conquerors.

He took Ohiyesa to a small plot of farming land in western South Dakota and began teaching him to be a new type of warrior. He sent him off to white schools with the admonition that "it is the same as if I sent you on your first warpath. I shall expect you to conquer."

Thus was born Charles Alexander Eastman, the Santee Sioux child of the woodlands and prairies who would go on to become the adviser to presidents and an honored member of New England society.

Ohiyesa, or Eastman, went to Beloit College where he learned English and immersed himself in the culture and ways of the white world. Upon graduation he went east. He attended Dartmouth College, then was accepted into medical school at Boston University, which he completed in 1890. He returned to his native Midwest to work among his own people as a physician on the Pine Ridge reservation, but became disenchanted with the corruption of the U.S. government and its Indian agents. After a short-lived effort to establish a private medical practice in St. Paul, Minnesota, he turned his focus back to the issue of Indian-white relations.

For the next twenty-five years, he was involved in various efforts to build bridges of understanding between the Indians and non-Indian people of America. He worked first for the YMCA, then served as an attorney for his people in Washington, then returned to South Dakota to spend three years as physician for the Sioux at Crow Creek.

In 1903 he went back to Massachusetts and devoted himself to bringing the voice of the Indian into the American intellectual arena. He became deeply involved in the Boy Scout program, believing it was the best way to give non-Indian American youth a sense of the wonder and values that he had learned growing up in the wild.

Eventually, with the help of his wife, he established a camp of his own in New Hampshire in which he tried to recreate the experience of Sioux education and values for non-Indian children.

But financial troubles and the fundamentally irreconcilable differences between Indian culture and white civilization ultimately took their toll. In 1918 he and his white wife separated, and in 1921 he left New England for good. He continued to believe that the way of civilization was the way of the future, but he had lost much of his faith in its capacity to speak to the higher moral and spiritual vision of humanity. He returned again to his native forests of the Midwest, devoting more time to his traditional ways, often going into the woods alone for months at a time.

But he never ceased believing that the two cultures that had clashed so tragically on the soil of the American continent somehow had to become one if there ever was to be a true America with an honest and indigenous soul. Even though he had come to believe that white civilization was, at heart, "a system of life based on trade," he still felt that it was the task of the best people, both Indian and non-Indian, to help America find a shared vision. As he said at the end of his autobiography, *From Deep Woods to Civilization*, "I am an Indian; and while I have learned much from civilization, for which I am grateful, I have never lost my Indian sense of right and justice. I am for development and progress along social and spiritual lines, rather than those of commerce, nationalism, or efficiency. Nevertheless, so long as I live, I am an American."

As an observer of Indian life, Ohiyesa was unlike any other. He was at once completely secure in his Indian identity, yet gave himself over completely to the search for meaning within the context of a European America. He tried with his whole heart and spirit to believe in the wisdom of each of the ways he had learned. If there was struggle, it was because the two ways coexisted so uneasily within one person.

Though he lamented the passing of the Indian ways, he accepted it as the workings of the Great Mystery, and set himself to the dual task of bringing the ways of the whites to the Indians and the ways of the Indians to the whites. He never lost his grounding in his traditional ways, even while exploring the intricacies of "the Christ Ideal" and dining with presidents. He was ever the observer, journeying ever deeper into the ways of white culture, trying, as his grandmother had always instructed him, "to follow a new trail to the point of knowing."

The writings he has left are the documents of that journey, crafted by a man with a warrior's heart, an orator's tongue, and human spirit of such dignity that it transcends boundaries of race and belief.

It is with a great sense of honor and pride that I place this compilation of his writings before you. Ohiyesa is a man to whom I would entrust my son or my country. After you have read his words, you will understand why.

Kent Nerburn
Bemidji, Minnesota 1993

Foreword

"We also have a religion which has been given to our forefathers, and has been handed down to us their children. It teaches us to be thankful, to be united, and to love one another! We never quarrel about religion."

Thus spoke the great Seneca orator, Red Jacket, in his superb reply to Missionary Cram more than a century ago, and I have often heard the same thought expressed by my countrymen.

I have attempted to paint the religious life of the typical American Indian as it was before we knew the white race. I have long wished to do this, because I cannot find that it has ever been seriously, adequately, and sincerely done. Our religion is the last thing about us that the person of another race will ever understand.

First, we Indians do not speak of these deep matters so long as we believe in them, and those of us who have ceased to believe speak inaccurately and slightingly.

Second, even if we can be induced to speak, the racial and religious prejudice of the other stands in the way of any sympathetic comprehension.

Third, practically all existing studies on this subject have been made during the transition period, when the original beliefs and philosophy of the native American were already undergoing rapid disintegration.

There are to be found here and there superficial accounts of strange customs and ceremonies, of which the symbolism or inner meaning was largely hidden from the observer; and there has been a great deal of material collected in recent years which is without value because it is modern and hybrid, inextricably mixed with Biblical legend and Caucasian philosophy. Some of it has even been invented for commercial purposes. Find an Indian who is more concerned with profit than his heritage, and he will possibly provide you with sacred songs, a mythology, and folklore to order!

My writings do not pretend to be a scientific treatise. They are as true as I can make them to my childhood teaching and ancestral ideals, but from the human, not the ethnological stand-point. I have not cared to pile up more dry bones, but to clothe them with flesh and blood. So much that has been written by strangers of our ancient faith and worship treats it mainly as a matter of curiosity. I should like to emphasize its universal quality, its personal appeal!

The first missionaries who came among us were good men, but they were imbued with the narrowness of their age. They branded us as pagans and devil-worshipers, and demanded that we renounce our gods as false. They even told us that we were eternally lost unless we adopted their faith and all its symbols.

We of the twentieth century know better. We know that all religious aspiration, all sincere worship, can have but one source and goal. We know that the God of the educated and the God of the child, the God of the civilized and the God of the primitive, is after all the same God; and that this God does not measure our differences, but embraces all who live rightly and humbly on the earth.

Ohiyesa (Charles Alexander Eastman)

The Soul of an Indian

*Is there not something worthy of perpetuation
in our Indian spirit of democracy, where Earth,
our mother, was free to all, and no one sought
to impoverish or enslave his neighbor?*

Ohiyesa

1

The Ways of the Spirit

We do not chart and measure the vast field of nature or express her wonders in the terms of science; on the contrary, we see miracles on every hand — the miracle of life in seed and egg, the miracle of death in a lightning flash and in the swelling deep!

THE GREAT MYSTERY

The attitude of the American Indian toward the Eternal, the Great Mystery that surrounds and embraces us, is as simple as it is exalted. To us it is the supreme conception, bringing with it the fullest measure of joy and satisfaction possible in this life.

The worship of the Great Mystery is silent, solitary, free from all self-seeking.

It is silent, because all speech is of necessity feeble and imperfect; therefore the souls of our ancestors ascended to God in wordless adoration.

It is solitary, because we believe that God is nearer to us in solitude, and there are no priests authorized to come between us and our Maker. None can exhort or confess or in any way meddle with the religious experience of another. All of us are created children of God, and all stand erect, conscious of our divinity. Our faith cannot be formulated in creeds, nor forced upon any who are unwilling to receive it; hence there is no preaching, proselytizing, nor persecution, neither are there any scoffers or atheists.

Our religion is an attitude of mind, not a dogma.

THE TEMPLE OF NATURE

There are no temples or shrines among us save those of nature. Being children of nature, we are intensely poetical. We would deem it sacrilege to build a house for The One who may be met face to face in the mysterious, shadowy aisles of the primeval forest, or on the sunlit bosom of virgin

prairies, upon dizzy spires and pinnacles of
naked rock, and in the vast jeweled vault of the
night sky! A God who is enrobed in filmy veils of
cloud, there on the rim of the visible world
where our Great-Grandfather Sun kindles his
evening camp-fire; who rides upon the rigorous
wind of the north, or breathes forth spirit upon
fragrant southern airs, whose war canoe is
launched upon majestic rivers and inland seas —
such a God needs no lesser cathedral.

THE POWER OF SILENCE

We first Americans mingle with our pride an ex-
ceptional humility. Spiritual arrogance is foreign
to our nature and teaching. We never claimed that
the power of articulate speech is proof of superi-
ority over "dumb creation"; on the other hand, it
is to us a perilous gift.

We believe profoundly in silence — the sign
of a perfect equilibrium. Silence is the absolute
poise or balance of body, mind, and spirit. Those
who can preserve their selfhood ever calm and
unshaken by the storms of existence — not a leaf,
as it were, astir on the tree; not a ripple upon the

3

shining pool — those, in the mind of the person of nature, possess the ideal attitude and conduct of life.

If you ask us, "What is silence?" we will answer, "It is the Great Mystery. The holy silence is God's voice."

If you ask, "What are the fruits of silence?" we will answer, "They are self-control, true courage or endurance, patience, dignity, and reverence. Silence is the cornerstone of character."

"Guard your tongue in youth," said the old chief, Wabasha, "and in age you may mature a thought that will be of service to your people."

THE PRESENCE OF SPIRIT

Naturally magnanimous and open-minded, we have always preferred to believe that the Spirit of God is not breathed into humans alone, but that the whole created universe shares in the immortal perfection of its Maker.

The elements and majestic forces in nature — lightning, wind, water, fire, and frost — are regarded with awe as spiritual powers, but always secondary and intermediate in character. We believe that the spirit pervades all creation and that every creature possesses a soul in some degree, though not necessarily a soul conscious of itself. The tree, the waterfall, the grizzly bear, each is an embodied Force, and as such an object of reverence.

We Indians love to come into sympathy and spiritual communion with our brothers and sisters of the animal kingdom, whose inarticulate souls hold for us something of the sinless purity that we attribute to the innocent and irresponsible child. We have a faith in their instincts, as in a mysterious wisdom given from above; and while we humbly accept the sacrifice of their bodies to preserve our own, we pay homage to their spirits in prescribed prayers and offerings.

POVERTY AND SIMPLICITY

We original Americans have generally been despised by our white conquerors for our poverty and simplicity. They forget, perhaps, that our religion forbade the accumulation of wealth and the enjoyment of luxury. To us, as to other spiritually-minded people in every age and race, the love of possessions is a snare, and the burdens of a complex society a source of needless peril and temptation.

It is simple truth that we Indians did not, so long as our native philosophy held sway over our minds, either envy or desire to imitate the splendid achievements of the white race. In our own thought we rose superior to them! We scorned them, even as a lofty spirit absorbed in its own task rejects the soft beds, the luxurious food, the pleasure-worshipping dalliance of a rich neighbor. It was clear to us that virtue and happiness are independent of these things, if not incompatible with them.

Furthermore, it was the rule of our life to share the fruits of our skill and success with our less fortunate brothers and sisters. Thus we kept our spirits free from the clog of pride, avarice, or envy, and carried out, as we believed, the divine decree — a matter profoundly important to us.

NATURE AND SOLITUDE

As children of nature, we have always looked upon the concentration of population as the prolific mother of all evils, moral no less than physical. It was not, then, wholly from ignorance or improvidence that we failed to establish permanent towns and to develop a material civilization. We have always believed that food is good, while surfeit kills, that love is good, but lust destroys; and not less dreaded than the pestilence following upon crowded and unsanitary dwellings is the loss of spiritual power inseparable from too close contact with one's fellow men.

All who have lived much out of doors, whether Indian or otherwise, know that there is a magnetic and powerful force that accumulates in solitude but is quickly dissipated by life in a crowd. Even our enemies have recognized that for a certain innate power and self-poise, wholly independent of circumstances, the American Indian is unsurpassed among the races.

THE IMPORTANCE OF PRAYER

Prayer — the daily recognition of the Unseen and the Eternal — is our one inevitable duty.

We Indian people have traditionally divided mind into two parts — the spiritual mind and the

7

physical mind. The first — the spiritual mind — is concerned only with the essence of things, and it is this we seek to strengthen by spiritual prayer, during which the body is subdued by fasting and hardship. In this type of prayer there is no beseeching of favor or help.

The second, or physical, mind, is lower. It is concerned with all personal or selfish matters, like success in hunting or warfare, relief from sickness, or the sparing of a beloved life. All ceremonies, charms, or incantations designed to secure a benefit or to avert a danger are recognized as emanating from the physical self.

The rites of this physical worship are wholly symbolic; we may have sundances and other ceremonies, but the Indian no more worships the sun than the Christian worships the cross. In our view, the Sun and the Earth are the parents of all organic life. And, it must be admitted, in this our thinking is scientific truth as well as poetic metaphor.

For the Sun, as the universal father, sparks the principle of growth in nature, and in the patient and fruitful womb of our mother, the Earth, are hidden embryos of plants and men. Therefore our reverence and love for the Sun and the Earth are really an imaginative extension of our love for our immediate parents, and with this feeling of filial devotion is joined a willingness to appeal to them for such good gifts as we may desire. This is the material or physical prayer.

But, in a broader sense, our whole life is prayer because every act of our life is, in a very real sense, a religious act. Our daily devotions are more important to us than food.

We wake at daybreak, put on our moccasins and step down to the water's edge. Here we throw handfuls of clear, cold water into our face, or plunge in bodily.

After the bath, we stand erect before the advancing dawn, facing the sun as it dances upon the horizon, and offer our unspoken prayer. Our mate may proceed or follow us in our devotions, but never accompanies us. Each soul must meet the morning sun, the new sweet earth, and the Great Silence alone.

Whenever, in the course of our day, we might come upon a scene that is strikingly beautiful or sublime — the black thundercloud with the rainbow's glowing arch above the mountain; a white waterfall in the heart of a green gorge; a vast prairie tinged with the blood-red of sunset — we pause for an instant in the attitude of worship.

We recognize the spirit in all creation, and believe that we draw spiritual power from it. Our respect for the immortal part of our brothers and sisters, the animals, often leads us so far as to lay out the body of any game we catch and decorate the head with symbolic paint or feathers. We then stand before it in an attitude of prayer, holding up the pipe that contains our sacred tobacco, as a gesture that we have freed with honor the spirit of our brother or sister, whose body we were compelled to take to sustain our own life.

When food is taken, the woman murmurs a "grace" — an act so softly and unobtrusively performed that one who does not know the custom usually fails to catch the whisper: "Spirit, partake!"

As her husband receives his bowl or plate, he likewise murmurs his invocation to the spirit. When he becomes an old man, he loves to make a particular effort to prove his gratitude. He cuts off the choicest morsel of the meat and casts it into the fire — the purest and most ethereal element.

Thus we see no need for the setting apart one day in seven as a holy day, since to us all days belong to God.

THE APPRECIATION OF BEAUTY

In the appreciation of beauty, which is closely akin to religious feeling, the American Indian stands alone. In accord with our nature and beliefs, we do not pretend to imitate the inimitable, or to reproduce exactly the work of the Great Artist. That which is beautiful must not be trafficked with, but must only be revered and adored.

I have seen in our midsummer celebrations cool arbors built of fresh-cut branches for council and dance halls, while those who attended decked themselves with leafy boughs, carrying shields and fans of the same, and even making wreaths for their horses' necks. But, strange to say, they seldom make free use of flowers. I once asked the reason for this.

"Why," said one, "the flowers are for our souls to enjoy; not for our bodies to wear. Leave them alone and they will live out their lives and reproduce themselves as the Great Gardener intended.

He planted them; we must not pluck them, for it would be selfish to do so."

This is the spirit of the original American. We hold nature to be the measure of consummate beauty, and we consider its destruction to be a sacrilege.

I once showed a party of Sioux chiefs the sights of Washington, and endeavored to impress them with the wonderful achievements of civilization. After visiting the Capitol and other famous buildings, we passed through the Corcoran Art Gallery, where I tried to explain how the white man valued this or that painting as a work of genius and a masterpiece of art.

"Ah!" exclaimed an old man, "such is the strange philosophy of the white man! He hews down the forest that has stood for centuries in its pride and grandeur, tears up the bosom of Mother Earth, and causes the silvery watercourses to waste and vanish away. He ruthlessly disfigures God's own pictures and monuments, and then daubs a flat surface with many colors, and praises his work as a masterpiece!"

Here we have the root of the failure of the Indian to approach the "artistic" standard of the civilized world. It lies not in our lack of creative imagination — for in this quality we are born artists — it lies rather in our point of view. Beauty, in our eyes, is always fresh and living, even as God, the Great Mystery, dresses the world anew at each season of the year.

THE MIRACLE OF THE ORDINARY

We Indians have always been clear thinkers within the scope of our understanding, but cause and effect have not formed the basis for our thinking. We do not chart and measure the vast field of nature or express her wonders in the terms of science; on the contrary, we see miracles on every hand — the miracle of life in seed and egg, the miracle of death in a lightning flash and in the swelling deep!

Nothing of the marvelous can astonish us — a beast could speak or the sun stand still. The virgin birth seems scarcely more miraculous than is the birth of every child that comes into the world, and the miracle of the loaves and fishes excites no greater wonder than the harvest that springs from a single ear of corn.

Let us not forget that even for the most contemporary thinker, who sees a majesty and grandeur in natural law, science cannot explain everything. We all still have to face the ultimate miracle — the origin and principle of life. This is the supreme mystery that is the essence of worship and without which there can be no religion. In the presence of this mystery all peoples must take an attitude much like that of the Indian, who beholds with awe the Divine in all creation.

2

The Ways of the People

Let those I serve express their thanks according to their own upbringing and sense of honor.

THE TEACHING OF CHILDREN

It is commonly supposed that there was no systematic means of education for Indian children. Nothing could be further from the truth. All the customs of our people were held to be divinely instituted, and customs involving the training of children were scrupulously adhered to and transmitted from one generation to another.

It is true that we had no schoolhouses, no books, no regular school hours. Our children were trained in the natural way — they kept in close contact with the natural world. In this way, they found themselves and became conscious of their relationship to all of life. The spiritual world was real to them, and the splendor of life stood out above all else. And beyond all, and in all, was seen to dwell the Great Mystery, unsolved and unsolvable, except in those things that it is good for one's spirit to know.

We taught our children by both example and instruction, but with emphasis on example, because all learning is a dead language to one who gets it secondhand. Our physical training was thorough and intelligent, while as to the moral and spiritual side of our teaching, I am not afraid to compare it with that of any race.

We conceived the art of teaching as, first and foremost, the development of personality; and we considered the fundamentals of education to be love of the Great Mystery, love of nature, and love of people and country.

THE GREAT SONG OF CREATION

Our education begins in our mother's womb. Her attitude and secret meditations are such as to instill into the receptive soul of the unborn child the love of the Great Mystery and a sense of kinship with all creation.

A pregnant Indian woman often chooses one of the great individuals of her family and tribe as a model for her child. This hero is daily called to mind. She gathers from tradition all of his noted deeds and daring exploits, and rehearses them to herself when alone. In order that the impression might be more distinct, she avoids company. She isolates herself as much as possible, and wanders prayerful in the stillness of the great woods, or on the bosom of the untrodden prairie, not thought-lessly, but with an eye to the impressions received from the grand and beautiful scenery.

To her poetic mind the imminent birth of her child prefigures the advent of a great spirit — a hero, or the mother of heroes — a thought conceived in the virgin breast of primeval nature, and dreamed out in a hush broken only by the sighing of the pine tree or the thrilling orchestra of a distant waterfall.

And when the day of her days in her life dawns — the day in which there is to be a new life, the miracle of whose making has been entrusted to her — she seeks no human aid. She has been trained and prepared in body and mind for this, her holiest duty, ever since she can remember.

She meets the ordeal of childbirth alone, where no curious or pitying eyes might embarrass her; where all nature says to her spirit: "It is love! It is love! The fulfilling of life!"

When, at last, a sacred voice comes to her out of the silence, and a pair of eyes open upon her in the wilderness, she knows with joy that she has borne well her part in the great song of creation!

Presently she returns to the camp, carrying the mysterious, the holy, the dearest bundle! She feels the endearing warmth of it and hears its soft breathing. It is still a part of herself, since both are nourished by the same mouthful, and no look of a lover could be sweeter than its deep and trusting gaze.

THE CHILD'S FIRST LESSON

The Indian mother has not only the experience of her mother and grandmother, and the accepted rules of her people for a guide, but she humbly seeks to learn a lesson from ants, bees, spiders, beavers, and badgers. She studies the family life of the birds, so exquisite in its emotional intensity and its patient devotion, until she seems to feel the universal mother-heart beating in her own breast.

She continues her spiritual teaching, at first silently — a mere pointing of the index finger to nature — then in whispered songs, bird-like, at morning and evening. To her and to the child the birds are real people, who live very close to the Great Mystery. The murmuring trees breathe its presence; the falling waters chant its praise.

If the child should chance to be fretful, the mother raises her hand. "Hush! Hush!" she cautions it tenderly, "The spirits may be disturbed!" She bids it be still and listen — listen to the silver voice of the aspen, or the clashing cymbals of the birch; and at night she points to the heavenly blazed trail through nature's galaxy of splendor to nature's God. Silence, love, reverence — this is the trinity of first lessons, and to these she later adds generosity, courage, and chastity.

In due time children take of their own accord the attitude of prayer, and speak reverently of the Powers. They feel that all living creatures are blood brothers and sisters; the storm wind is to them a messenger of the Great Mystery.

THE ROLE OF THE ELDERS

At the age of about eight years, if her child is a boy, the mother turns him over to the father for more disciplined training. If the child is a girl, she is from this time much under the guardianship of her grandmother, who is considered the most dignified protector for the maiden.

The distinctive work of the grandparents is that of acquainting the children with the traditions and beliefs of the nation. The grandparents are old and wise. They have lived and achieved. They are dedicated to the service of the young, as their teachers and advisers, and the young in turn regard them with love and reverence. In them the Indian recognizes the natural and truest teachers of the child.

It is reserved for them to repeat the time-hallowed tales with dignity and authority, so as to lead the child into the inheritance of the stored-up wisdom and experience of the race.

The long winter evenings are considered the proper time for the learning of those traditions that have their roots in the past and lead back to the source of all things. And since the subjects lay half in the shadow of mystery, they have to be taken up at night, the proper realm of mysticism.

Through the telling of these tales, the grandparents inspire love of heroes, pride of ancestry, and devotion to country and people. But these tales do more than enlarge the mind and stimulate the imagination. They furnish the best of memory training, as the child is required to remember and repeat them one by one.

There was usually some old man whose gifts as a storyteller and keeper of wisdom spread his fame far beyond the limits of his immediate family. In his home, at the time of the winter camp, the children of the band were accustomed to gather with more or less regularity.

This was our nearest approach to a school of the woods, and the teacher received his pay not only in gifts of food and other comforts, but chiefly in the love and respect of the village.

A LIFE OF SERVICE

The public position of the Indian has always been entirely dependent upon our private virtue. We are never permitted to forget that we do not live to ourselves alone, but to our tribe and clan. Every child, from the first days of learning, is a public servant in training.

In our traditional ways, the child is kept ever before the public eye, from birth onward. The birth would be announced by the tribal herald, accompanied by a distribution of presents to the old and needy. The same thing would occur when the child took its first step, spoke its first word, had its ears pierced, shot his first game.

Not a step in the child's development was overlooked as an excuse to bring it before the public by giving a feast in its honor. Thus the child's progress was known to the whole clan as to a larger family, and the child grew to adulthood with a sense of reputation to sustain.

At such feasts the parents often gave so generously to the needy that they almost impoverished themselves, thereby setting an example to the child of self-denial for the public good. In this way, children were shown that big-heartedness, generosity, courage, and self-denial are the qualifications of a public servant, and from the cradle we sought to follow this ideal.

The young boy was encouraged to enlist early in the public service, and to develop a wholesome ambition for the honors of a leader and feastmaker, which could never be his unless he proved truthful and generous, as well as brave, and ever mindful of his personal chastity and honor.

As to the young girls, it was the loving parents' pride to have their daughters visit the unfortunate and the helpless, carry them food, comb their hair, and mend their garments. The name "Wenonah," bestowed upon the eldest daughter, means "Bread Giver," or "Charitable One," and a girl who failed in her charitable duties was held to be unworthy of the name.

THE BEAUTY OF GENEROSITY

It has always been our belief that the love of possessions is a weakness to be overcome. Its appeal is to the material part, and if allowed its way it will in time disturb the spiritual balance for which we all strive.

Therefore we must early learn the beauty of generosity. As children we are taught to give what we prize most, that we may taste the happiness of giving; at an early age we are made the family giver of alms. If a child is inclined to be grasping, or to cling too strongly to possessions, legends are related that tell of the contempt and disgrace falling on those who are ungenerous and mean.

Public giving is a part of every important ceremony. It properly belongs to the celebration of birth, marriage, and death, and is observed whenever it is desired to do special honor to any person or event.

Upon such occasions it is common to literally give away all that one has to relatives, to guests of another tribe or clan, but above all to the poor and the aged, from whom we can hope for no return.

Finally, the gift to the Great Mystery, the religious offering, may be of little value in itself, but to the giver's own thought it should carry the meaning and reward of true sacrifice.

ORDER, ETIQUETTE, AND DECORUM

No one who is at all acquainted with us in our homes can deny that we Indians are a polite people.

There are times when we indulge in boisterous mirth — indeed, I have often spent an entire evening at an Indian fireside laughing until I could laugh no more — but the general rule of behavior is gravity and decorum. The enforced intimacy of living in close quarters would soon become intolerable were it not for these instinctive reserves and delicacies; this unfailing respect for the established place and possessions of every other member of the family circle; this habitual quiet, order, and decorum.

Only the aged, who have journeyed far, are in a manner exempt from ordinary rules. Advancing years have earned them freedom, not only from the burden of laborious and dangerous tasks, but from those restrictions of custom and etiquette that are religiously observed by all others.

The old men and women are privileged to say what they please and how they please, without contradiction, while the hardships and bodily infirmities that of necessity fall to their lot are softened so far as may be by universal consideration and attention.

But for the rest of us, a soft, low voice has always been considered an excellent thing, in a man as well as in a woman. Even the warrior who inspired the greatest terror in the hearts of his enemies was, as a rule, a man of the most exemplary gentleness, and almost feminine refinement, among his family and friends. And though we are capable of strong and durable feeling, we are not demonstrative in our affection at any time, especially in the presence of guests or strangers.

It is a rule of the Indian home that the grandfather is master of ceremonies at all times. He is spokesman for the family if a stranger enters. If he is absent, the father or the husband speaks; all others may only smile in greeting. If both men are absent, the grandmother is spokeswoman; if she is away, the mother or the wife speaks, with as much dignity as modesty. If no older person is at home, the eldest son or daughter greets the guest, but if they have no brother to speak for them, and an entire stranger enters, the girls may properly observe silence. The stranger should explain the reason for the intrusion.

In the presence of a guest, promiscuous laughing or a careless attitude are not permitted. Rigid decorum and respectful silence are observed, and if any children are present, they must not stare at the stranger. All noisy play and merriment must be kept within familiar family circles, except on the occasion of certain games and dances.

The serving of food is always orderly and polite. Guests are offered food at whatever hour of the day they may appear. The mother of the family serves first the guest, if any, then her father, her husband, her mother, the children in order of age, and, herself last of all. Each person returns the empty dish to her with appropriate words of thanks.

Simple as they seem, these rules and conventions have stood the test of time and are universally respected. In such ways is the natural life of the Indian saved from rudeness and disorder.

THE MORAL STRENGTH
OF WOMEN

In the woman is vested the standard of morals of our people. She is the silent but telling power behind all of life's activities.

She rules undisputed in her own domain. The children belong to her clan, not to the clan of the father. She holds all the family property, and the honor of the house is in her hands. All virtue is entrusted to her, and her position is recognized by all.

Possessed of true feminine dignity and modesty, she is expected to be the equal of her mate in physical endurance and skill, and to share equally in the arduous duties of daily life. But she is expected to be superior in spiritual insight.

She is the spiritual teacher of the child, as well as its tender nurse, and she brings its developing soul before the Great Mystery as soon as she is aware of its coming. It is her responsibility to endow her child with nature's gifts and powers, for we believe that from the moment of conception to the end of the second year, it is her spiritual influence that counts for most.

There is nothing artificial about her person, and very little insincerity in her character. Her early and consistent training, the definiteness of her vocation, and, above all, her profoundly religious attitude gives her a strength and poise that cannot be overcome by ordinary misfortune.

It is my belief that no woman of any race has ever come closer to universal motherhood. She is, in fact, the moral salvation of our people.

THE SACREDNESS OF HONOR

A sense of honor pervades all aspects of Indian life.

Orphans and the aged are invariably cared for, not only by their next of kin, but by the whole clan. The man who is a skillful hunter, and whose wife is alive to her opportunities, makes many feasts, to which he is careful to invite the older men of his clan. He recognizes that they have outlived their period of greatest activity, and now love nothing so well as to eat in good company and live over their past.

He sets no price upon either his property or his labor. His generosity is limited only by his strength. He regards it as an honor to be selected for a difficult or dangerous service, and would think it a shame to ask for any other reward, saying rather: "Let those I serve express their thanks according to their own upbringing and sense of honor."

He is always ready to undertake the impossible, or to impoverish himself for the sake of a friend.

Where the other person is regarded more than the self, duty is sweeter and more inspiring, patriotism more sacred, and friendship is a pure and eternal bond.

THE HONOR OF WARFARE

The common impression that the Indian is naturally cruel and revengeful is entirely opposed to our philosophy and training. Warfare was regarded largely as sort of a game, undertaken in order to develop the manly qualities of our youth.

It was the coming of white traders with their guns, knives, and whiskey, that roused the revengeful tendencies of the Indian. In our natural state we were neither mean nor deceitful. It is true that men like King Philip, Weatherford, and Little Crow lifted their hands against the white man. But their fathers, Massasoit, Attackullakulla, and Wabasha, had held out their hands with gifts.

In our natural state, it was the degree of risk that brought honor, rather than the number slain, and a brave man would mourn thirty days, with blackened face and loosened hair, for the enemy whose life had been taken.

And while the spoils of war were allowed, this did not extend to appropriation of the other's territory, nor was there any wish to overthrow another nation and enslave its people.

Indeed, if an enemy honored us with a call, his trust was not misplaced, and he went away convinced that he had met with a royal host! Our honor was the guarantee for his safety, so long as he remained within the camp.

It was also a point of honor in the old days to treat a captive with kindness. I remember well an instance that occurred when I was very small.

My uncle brought home two young Ojibwe women who had been captured in a fight between my people and the Ojibwe. Since none of the Sioux war party had been killed, the women received sympathy and were tenderly treated by the Sioux women. They were apparently very happy, although of course they felt deeply the losses sustained at the time of their capture, and they did not fail to show their appreciation of the kindnesses received at our hands.

As I recall now the remarks made by one of them at the time of their final release, they appear to me quite remarkable. They lived in my grandmother's family for two years, and were then returned to their people at a great peace council of the two nations. When they were about to leave, the elder of the two sisters embraced my grandmother, and then spoke somewhat as follows:

"You are a brave woman and a true mother. I understand now why your son bravely conquered our band, and took my sister and myself as captive. I hated him at first, but now I admire him, because he did just what my father, my brother, or my husband would have done had they opportunity. He did even more. He saved us from the tomahawks of his fellow warriors, and brought us to his home to know a noble and a brave woman.

"I shall never forget your many favors shown to us. But I must go. I belong to my tribe and I shall return to them. I will endeavor to be a true woman also, and to teach my boys to be generous warriors like your son."

Her sister chose to remain among the Sioux all her life, and she married one of our young men.

"I shall make the Sioux and the Ojibwe," she said, "to be as brothers."

But it is perhaps Chief Joseph, who conducted that masterly retreat of eleven hundred miles, burdened with his women and children, the old men and the wounded, who best embodied the honor of warfare. Surely he had reason to hate the race who had driven him from his home. Yet it is a fact that while Joseph was in retreat, when he met white visitors and travelers, some of whom were women, he allowed them to pass unharmed, and in at least one instance let them have horses to help them on their way.

RESPECT FOR JUSTICE

Before there were any cities on this continent, before there were bridges to span the Mississippi, before the great network of railroads was even dreamed of, we Indian people had councils which gave their decisions in accordance with the highest ideal of human justice.

Though the occurrence of murder was rare, it was a grave offense, to be atoned for as the council might decree. Often it happened that the slayer was called upon to pay the penalty with his own life.

In such cases, the murderer made no attempt to escape or evade justice. That the crime was committed in the depths of the forest or at dead of night, witnessed by no human eye, made no difference to his mind. He was thoroughly convinced that all is known to the Great Mystery, and hence did not hesitate to give himself up, to stand trial by the old and wise men of the victim's clan.

Even his own family and clan might by no means attempt to excuse or to defend him. But his judges took all the known circumstances into consideration, and if it appeared that he slew in self-defense, or that the provocation was severe, he might be set free after a thirty days' period of mourning in solitude. This ceremonial mourning was a sign of reverence for the departed spirit.

If there were no circumstances justifying the slaying, the murdered man's next of kin were authorized to take the murderer's life. If they refrained from doing so, as often happened, he remained an outcast from the clan.

It is well remembered that Crow Dog, who killed the Sioux chief, Spotted Tail, in 1881 calmly surrendered himself and was tried and convicted by the courts in South Dakota.

The cause of his act was a solemn commission received from his people thirty years earlier. At that time, Spotted Tail had usurped the chieftainship of his people with the aid of the U.S. military. Crow Dog was under a vow to slay the chief, in case he ever disgraced the name of the Brule Sioux.

There is no doubt that Spotted Tail had committed crimes both public and private, having been guilty of misuse of office as well as of gross offense against morality. Therefore, his death was not a matter of personal vengeance, but of just retribution.

A few days before Crow Dog was to be executed, he asked permission to visit his home and say farewell to his wife and twin boys, then nine or ten years old. Strange to say, the request was granted, and the condemned man was sent home under escort of the deputy sheriff, who remained at the Indian agency, merely telling his prisoner to report there on the following day.

When Crow Dog did not appear at the time set, the sheriff dispatched the Indian police after him. They did not find him, and his wife simply said that he had desired to ride alone to the prison, and would reach there on the day appointed. All doubt was removed the next day by a telegram from Rapid City, two hundred miles distant. It said, "Crow Dog has just reported here."

This incident drew public attention, with the unexpected result that the case was reopened, and Crow Dog was acquitted. He returned to his home and lived much respected among his people.

THE DISGRACE OF LYING AND THIEVERY

Such is the importance of our honor and our word that in the early days, lying was a capital offense. Because we believed that the deliberate liar is capable of committing any crime behind the screen of cowardly untruth and double dealing, the destroyer of mutual confidence was summarily put to death, that the evil might go no further.

Likewise, thievery was a disgrace, and if discovered, the name of "wamonon," or Thief, was fixed upon him forever as an unalterable stigma.

The only exception to the rule was in the case of food, which is always free to the hungry if there is none to offer it. Other protection than the moral law there could not be in an Indian community, where there were neither locks nor doors, and everything was open and of easy access to all comers.

FRIENDSHIP

Among our people, friendship is held to be the severest test of character.

It is easy, we think, to be loyal to family and clan, whose blood is in our own veins. Love between man and woman is founded on the mating instinct, and is not free from desire and self-seeking. But to have a friend, and to be true under any and all trials, is the truest mark of a man!

The highest type of friendship is the relation of "brother-friend" or "life-and-death" friend. This bond is between man and man; it is usually formed in early youth, and can only be broken by death.

It is the essence of comradeship and fraternal love, without thought of pleasure or gain, but rather for moral support and inspiration. Each vows to die for the other, if need be, and nothing is denied the brother-friend, but neither is anything required that is not in accord with the highest conception of the Indian mind.

BRAVERY AND COURAGE

As to our personal bravery and courage, no race can outdo us. Even our worst enemies, those who accuse us of treachery, blood-thirstiness, cruelty, and lust, have not denied our courage. But in their minds, our courage is ignorant, brutal, and fanatical. Our own conception of bravery makes of it a high moral virtue, for to us it consists not so much in aggressive self-assertion as in absolute self-control.

The brave man, we contend, yields neither to fear nor anger, desire nor agony. He is at all times master of himself; his courage rises to the heights of chivalry, patriotism, and real heroism.

The Creek war chief, Weatherford, was such a man. After Jackson had defeated the Creeks, he demanded Weatherford, dead or alive. The following night Weatherford presented himself at the general's tent, saying, "I am Weatherford. Do as you please with me. I would still be fighting you had I the warriors to fight with. But they no longer answer my call, for they are dead."

Crazy Horse, too, was a man of true bravery and honor. It was observed that when he pursued the enemy into their stronghold, as he was wont to do, he often refrained from killing, and simply struck them with a switch, showing that he did not fear their weapons nor care to waste his upon them.

"Let neither cold, hunger, nor pain, nor the fear of them, neither the bristling teeth of danger, nor the very jaws of death itself, prevent you from doing a good deed," said an old chief to a scout who was about to seek the buffalo in midwinter for the relief of his starving people. This was our pure and simple conception of courage.

THE REALITY OF PSYCHIC POWERS

It is well accepted that the Indian had well-developed psychic powers.

A Sioux prophet predicted the coming of the white man fully fifty years before the event, and even described accurately his garments and weapons. Before the steamboat was invented, another prophet of our race described the "fire boat" that would swim upon the mighty river, the Mississippi.

Some of us also seem to have a peculiar intuition for the locality of a grave. Those who possess this sensitivity often explain it by saying that they have received a communication from the spirit of the departed.

My own grandmother was one of these. As far back as I can remember, when camping in a strange country, my brother and I would search for and find human bones at the spot she had indicated to us as an ancient burial-place or the spot where a lone warrior had fallen. Of course, the outward signs of burial had long since been obliterated.

She had other remarkable premonitions or intuitions that I recall. I heard her speak of a peculiar sense in the breast, by which, as she said, she was advised of anything of importance concerning her absent children. Other native women have claimed a similar monitor, but I never heard of one who could interpret it with such accuracy.

We were once camping on Lake Manitoba when we received news that my uncle and his family had been murdered several weeks before at a fort some two hundred miles distant. While all our clan were wailing and mourning, my grandmother calmly bade them cease, saying that her son was approaching, and that they would see him shortly.

Although we had no other reason to doubt the ill tidings, it is a fact that my uncle came into camp two days after his reported death.

At another time, when I was fourteen years old, we had just left Fort Ellis on the Assiniboine River, and my youngest uncle had selected a fine spot for our night camp. It was already after sundown, but my grandmother became unaccountably nervous, and positively refused to pitch her tent.

So we reluctantly went on down the river, and camped after dark at a secluded place. The next day we learned that a family who were following close behind had stopped at the place first selected by my uncle, but were surprised in the night by a roving war-party, and all were massacred. This incident made a great impression on our people.

Many of us believe that one may be born more than once, and there are some who claim to have

41

full knowledge of a former incarnation. There are also those who believe in a "twin spirit" born into another tribe or race.

There once was a well-known Sioux war-prophet who lived in the middle of the last century, so that he is still remembered by the old men of his band. After he had reached middle age, he declared that he had a spirit brother among the Ojibwe, the ancestral enemies of the Sioux. He even named the band to which his brother belonged, and said that he also was a war-prophet among his people.

Upon one of their hunts along the border between the two tribes, the Sioux leader one evening called his warriors together, and solemnly declared to them that they were about to meet a like band of Ojibwe hunters, led by his spirit twin.

Since this was to be their first meeting since they were born as strangers, he earnestly begged the young men to resist the temptation to join battle with their tribal foes.

"You will know him at once," the prophet said to them, "for he will not only look like me in face and form, but he will display the same totem, and even sing my war songs!"

They sent out scouts, who soon returned with news of the approaching party. Then the leading men started with their peace-pipe for the Ojibwe camp, and when they were near at hand they fired three distinct volleys, a signal of their desire for a peaceful meeting. The response came in like manner, and they entered the camp with the peace pipe in the hands of the prophet.

Lo, the stranger prophet advanced to meet them, and the people were greatly struck with the resemblance between the two men, who met and embraced each other with unusual fervor.

It was quickly agreed by both parties that they should camp together for several days, and one evening the Sioux made a "warriors' feast" to which they invited many of the Ojibwe. The prophet asked his twin brother to sing one of his sacred songs, and behold, it was the very song that he himself was wont to sing.

No doubt many such stories were altered and shaded after the fact, and unquestionably, false prophets and conjurers abounded during the times of tribulation when the white races overtook our people. But I know that our people possessed remarkable powers of concentration and abstraction, and I believe that such nearness to nature as I have described keeps the spirit sensitive to impressions not commonly felt, and in touch with the unseen powers.

THE MEANING OF DEATH

Our attitude toward death, the test and background of life, is entirely consistent with our character and philosophy. Certainly we never doubt the immortal nature of the human soul or spirit, but neither do we care to speculate upon its probable state or condition in a future life.

The idea of a "happy hunting ground" is modern, and probably borrowed from or invented by the white man. In our original belief we were content to believe that the spirit which the Great Mystery breathed into us returns to the Creator who gave it, and that after it is freed from the body it is everywhere and pervades all nature.

Thus, death holds no terrors for us. We meet it with simplicity and perfect calm, seeking only an honorable end as our last gift to our family and descendants. Therefore we court death in battle but consider it disgraceful to be killed in a private quarrel. If we are dying at home, it is customary to have our bed be carried out of doors as the end approaches, so that our spirit may pass under the open sky.

Next to this, the matter that concerns us most is the parting with our dear ones, especially if we have any little children who must be left behind to suffer want. Our family affections are strong, so those of us left behind grieve intensely for those who pass, even though we have unbounded faith in a spiritual companionship and believe that the spirit of the departed lingers near the grave or "spirit bundle" for the consolation of friends, and is able to hear prayers.

Our outward signs of mourning for the dead are far more spontaneous and convincing than the correct and well-ordered black-clothed manners of civilization. Both men and women among us loosen our hair and cut it according to the degree of relationship or devotion.

Consistent with the ideal of sacrificing all personal beauty and adornment, we trim off likewise from the dress its fringes and ornaments, perhaps cut it short, or cut the robe or blanket in two.

Men blacken their faces, and widows or bereaved parents sometimes gash their arms and legs till they are covered with blood. Giving themselves up wholly to their grief, they are no longer concerned about any earthly possession, and often give away all that they have, even their beds and their home, to the first comers.

The wailing for the dead continues night and day to the point of utter voicelessness; it is a musical, weird, and heart-piercing sound, which has been compared to the "keening" of the Celtic mourner.

I recall a touching custom among us, which was designed to keep the memory of the departed near and warm in the bereaved household. A lock of hair of the beloved dead was wrapped in pretty clothing, something it was supposed that he or she would like to wear if living. This "spirit bundle," as it was called, was suspended from a tripod, and occupied a place of honor in the lodge. At every meal time, a dish of food was placed under it, and some person of the same sex and age as the one who once was must afterward be invited in to partake of the food. At the end of a year from the time of death, the relatives made a public feast and gave away the clothing and other gifts, while the lock of hair was interred with appropriate ceremonies.

Even the slaying of an enemy required proper respect for the dead. Though it was considered no sin to take the life of a man in battle, still, the slayer of the man was expected to mourn for thirty days, blackening his face and loosening his hair according to the custom. This ceremonial mourning was a sign of reverence for the departed spirit.

So much reverence was due the departed spirit that it was not customary with us even to name the dead aloud.

3

The Coming of the
White Ways

*Long before I heard of Christ or saw a white
man . . . I knew God. I perceived what goodness
is. I saw and loved what is really beautiful.
Civilization has not taught me anything better!*

THE EFFECT OF
THE WHITE RELIGION

Our transition from our natural life to the artificial life of civilization has resulted in great spiritual and moral loss.

In effect, the European who came among us
said, "You are a child. You cannot make or invent
anything. We have the only God, and He has

given us authority to teach and to govern all the peoples of the earth. In proof of this we have His Book, a supernatural guide, every word of which is true and binding. We are a chosen people — a superior race. We have a heaven with golden gates fenced in from all pagans and unbelievers, and a hell where the souls of such are tortured eternally. We are honorable, truthful, refined, religious, peaceful; we hate cruelty and injustice; our business is to educate, Christianize, and protect the rights and property of the weak and the un-civilized."

Those of us who listened to the preaching of the missionaries came to believe that the white man alone had a real God, and that the things which the Indian had previously held sacred were inventions of the devil. This undermined the very foundations of our philosophy. It very often did so without substituting the Christian philosophy, not because the innate qualities of the Christian philosophy were unworthy, but because the inconsistent behavior of its advocates made it hard for us to accept or understand.

A few of us did, in good faith, accept the white man's God. The black-robed preacher was like the Indian himself in seeking no soft things, and as he followed the fortunes of the tribes in the wilderness, the tribesmen learned to trust and to love him.

Then came other missionaries who had houses to sleep in, and gardens planted, and who hesitated to sleep in the Indian's wigwam or eat of his wild meat, but for the most part held themselves aloof and urged their own dress and ways upon their converts. These, too, had their following in due time.

But in the main it is true that while the Indian eagerly sought guns and gunpowder, knives and whiskey, a few articles of dress, and, later, horses, he did not of himself desire the white man's food, his houses, his books, his government, or his religion.

The two great "civilizers," after all, were whiskey and gunpowder, and from the hour we accepted these we had in reality sold our birthright, and all unconsciously consented to our own ruin.

Once we had departed from the broad democracy and pure idealism of our prime, and had undertaken to enter upon the world's game of competition, our rudder was unshipped, our compass lost, and the whirlwind and tempest of materialism and love of conquest tossed us to and fro like leaves in a wind.

THE HYPOCRISY OF THE CHRISTIANS AMONG US

There was undoubtedly much in primitive Christianity to appeal to the Indians, and Jesus' hard sayings to the rich and about the rich were entirely comprehensible to us. Yet the religion that we heard preached in churches and saw practiced by congregations, with its element of display and self-aggrandizement, its active proselytism, and its open contempt of all religions but its own, was for a long time extremely repellent.

I am reminded of a time when a missionary undertook to instruct a group of our people in the truth of his holy religion. He told them of the creation of the earth in six days, and of the fall of our first parents by eating an apple.

My people were courteous, and listened attentively; and after thanking the missionary, one man related in his own turn a very ancient tradition concerning the origin of maize. But the missionary plainly showed his disgust and disbelief, indignantly saying, "What I delivered to you were sacred truths, but this that you tell me is mere fable and falsehood!"

"My brother," gravely replied the offended Indian, "it seems that you have not been well grounded in the rules of civility. You saw that we, who practice these rules, believed your stories. Why, then, do you refuse to credit ours?"

Who may condemn our belief? Surely not the devout Catholic, or even the Protestant missionary who teaches Bible miracles as literal fact! The logical person must either deny all miracles or none, and our American Indian myths and hero stories are no less credible than those of the Hebrews of old.

Strange as it may seem, it is true that in our secret soul we despised the good men who came to convert and enlighten us! To our mind, the professionalism of the pulpit, the paid exhorter, the moneyed church, was an unspiritual and unedifying thing, and it was not until our spirit was broken and our moral and physical constitution undermined by trade, conquest, and strong drink, that the Christian missionaries obtained any real hold upon us.

Nor were its proselytism and hypocrisy the only elements in the alien religion that offended us. We found it shocking and almost incredible that among this race that claimed to be superior there were many who did not even pretend to profess the faith. Not only did they not profess it, but they stooped so low as to insult their God with profane and sacrilegious speech! In our own tongue the name of God was not spoken aloud, even with utmost reverence, much less lightly and irreverently.

More than this, even in those white men who professed religion we found much inconsistency of conduct. They spoke much of spiritual things, while seeking only the material. They bought and sold everything: time, labor, personal independence, the love of woman, and even the ministrations of their holy faith!

The higher and spiritual life, though first in theory, was clearly secondary, if not entirely neglected, in practice.

THE TRUE SPIRIT OF JESUS

This lust for money, power, and conquest did not escape moral condemnation at our hands, nor did we fail to contrast this conspicuous trait of the dominant race with the spirit of the meek and lowly Jesus.

I remember the words of one old battle-scarred warrior. I was at the time meeting with groups of young men — Sioux, Cheyenne, Cree, Ojibwe, and others — in log cabins or little frame chapels trying to set before them in simple language the life and character of the man Jesus.

The old warrior got up and said, "Why, we have followed this law you speak of for untold ages! We owned nothing, because everything is from the Creator. Food was free, land as free as sunshine and rain. Who has changed all this? The white man. And yet he says he is a believer in God! He does not seem to inherit any of the traits of his Father, nor does he follow the example set by his brother Christ."

Another of the older men, called upon for his views, kept a long silence. Finally, he said, "I have come to the conclusion that this Jesus was an

55

Indian. He was opposed to material acquisition and to great possessions. He was inclined to peace. He was as unpractical as any Indian and set no price upon his labor of love. These are not the principles upon which the white man has founded his civilization. It is strange that he could not rise to these simple principles which were so commonly observed among our people."

CHRISTIAN CIVILIZATION

In time we came to recognize that the drunkards and licentious among white men, with whom we too frequently came in contact, were condemned by the white man's religion as well, and must not be held to discredit it. But it was not so easy to overlook or to excuse national bad faith. When distinguished emissaries from the Father at Washington, some of them ministers of the Gospel and even bishops, came to the Indian nations, and pledged to us in solemn treaty the national honor, with prayer and mention of their God; and when such treaties, so made, were promptly and shamelessly broken, is it strange that the action should arouse not only anger, but contempt?

The historians of the white race admit that the Indian was never the first to repudiate his oath.

I confess I have wondered much that Christianity is not practiced by the very people who vouch for that wonderful conception of exemplary living. It appears that they are anxious to pass on their religion to all other races, but keep very little of it for themselves. I have not yet seen the meek inherit the earth, or the peacemakers receive high honor.

It is my personal belief, after thirty five years' experience of it, that there is no such thing as "Christian civilization." I believe that Christianity and modern civilization are opposed and irreconcilable, and that the spirit of Christianity and of our ancient religion is essentially the same.

LAMENT FOR A LOST VISION

Long before I ever heard of Christ or saw a white man, I had learned the essence of morality.

With the help of dear Nature herself, my grandmother taught me things simple but of mighty import.

I knew God. I perceived what goodness is. I saw and loved what is really beautiful. Civilization has not taught me anything better!

As a child, I understood how to give. I have forgotten that grace since I became civilized. I lived the natural life, whereas I now live the artificial.

Any pretty pebble was valuable to me then; every growing tree an object of reverence. Now I worship with the white man before a painted landscape whose value is estimated in dollars!

In this manner is the Indian rebuilt, as the natural rocks are ground to powder, and made into artificial blocks which may be built into the walls of modern society.

THE GIFT OF MY PEOPLE

I am an Indian; and while I have learned much from civilization, I have never lost my Indian sense of right and justice.

When I reduce civilization to its most basic terms, it becomes a system of life based on trade. Each man stakes his powers, the product of his labor, his social, political, and religious standing against his neighbor. To gain what? To gain control over his fellow workers, and the results of their labor.

Is there not something worthy of perpetuation in our Indian spirit of democracy, where Earth, our mother, was free to all, and no one sought to impoverish or enslave his neighbor? Where the good things of Earth were not ours to hold against our brothers and sisters, but were ours to use and enjoy together with them, and with whom it was our privilege to share?

Indeed, our contribution to our nation and the world is not to be measured in the material realm. Our greatest contribution has been spiritual and philosophical. Silently, by example only, in wordless patience, we have held stoutly to our native vision of personal faithfulness to duty and devotion to a trust. We have not advertised our faithfulness nor made capital of our honor.

But again and again we have proved our worth as citizens of this country by our constancy in the face of hardship and death. Prejudice and racial injustice have been no excuse for our breaking our word. This simplicity and fairness has cost us dear. It has cost us our land and our freedom, and even the extinction of our race as a separate and unique people.

But, as an ideal, we live and will live, not only in the splendor of our past, the poetry of our legends and art, not only in the interfusion of our blood with yours, and in our faithful adherence to the ideals of American citizenship, but in the living heart of the nation.

Afterword

If you are familiar with the works of Ohiyesa under his Anglicized name of Charles Alexander Eastman, or if you were expecting a new edition of his long-forgotten classic, *The Soul of the Indian*, this work will have come as a surprise.

This book is something different. It is a reconfiguration of his writings, chosen from a variety of sources, edited and woven together in a thematic narrative that gives voice to the spiritual vision that animated all his writing and speaking.

This was a delicate task, but one that I believe was necessary.

Ohiyesa lived and wrote at a time in which he had to distance himself from his native people, even to the point of appearing to be apart from them, in order to have credibility with a non-Indian readership that saw the Indian as almost less than human. As he put it, he had to "travel among Indians and study their nature as if I were not of the same race."

But this distance did not come without a cost. To watch him struggle for objectivity in his writings is to watch a man struggle with his heart. In one paragraph he will talk about the Indian people in objective terms, referring to them as "they" or "the native people," trying to appear as a disinterested, analytical observer. Then, in the very next paragraph, he will lose this distance and begin to refer to "we," as if the effort and the inner betrayal is too great for him to endure.

As he progressed through life, this bifurcation bothered him more and more. Day by day, step by step, he moved closer to the ways that had been taught to him by his uncle and his grandmother, until finally he retreated to the woodlands of his childhood and lived out his life amid the silence and the solitude of the forest. Charles Alexander Eastman, the interpreter, the physician, the counselor to presidents, had once again become Ohiyesa, son of Many Lightnings, and proud inheritor of his Santee heritage. He had completed the sacred circle of life by returning to the point from which he had begun.

In this compilation I am proud to complete that circle in his writing. I give him back his traditional name and his point of view as a member of the Dakota people. Specifically, this means I have changed the "they's" to "we's" where it was not unseemly to do so, and I have moved much of the past tense back into the present, so that the beliefs that in youth and age were so much a part of Ohiyesa's spiritual vision, once again are presented as his own.

This, I think, is a choice he would have applauded, and a choice I believe he himself would have made if he had been in the position to do so. It allows him for the first time, to speak from within his own race and within his own belief.

I have also made certain choices regarding language and usage in order to accommodate contemporary sensibilities.

Where appropriate, I have tried to make his language more gender inclusive. I have modified some language that today seems denigrating, such as the use of the term "savage" to describe the Indian. Though such language was in common use at the time, and often was meant more for descriptive purposes than as a value judgment, it rings harsh upon our ears and colors our attitude toward texts in which it appears. Likewise, I have rephrased passages in which Ohiyesa uses the "reservation Indian" as a symbol of lost Indian values. Today, the Indian who remains on the reservation very often has more opportunity to live his or her traditional values than the one who leaves. Accordingly, I have tried to cast such references in contemporary terms, using phrases such as "the Indian who has abandoned traditional values."

Finally, I have chosen selectively from among and within Ohiyesa's works. I have interpolated sentences from different sources, elided sentences and phrases, and tied thoughts from different sources together into common paragraphs. Here and there I have changed a noun to a pronoun or otherwise adjusted a sentence in order to make passages flow together smoothly. I have also combined paragraphs into common text without ellipses or reference notes.

Normally I would shy from such editorial manipulations. But Ohiyesa was a poet of the spirit, not a scholar. As he said in his Foreword to *The Soul of the Indian*, "My little book does not pretend to be a scientific treatise . . . I have not cared to pile up more dry bones, but to clothe them with flesh and blood. . . ."

By gathering his words from various sources, and making them flow together, I have attempted to take the dry bones of a time-bound text, clothe it with flesh and blood, and use his own words to reveal the richness of his spiritual vision. I have attempted, in his words, "to emphasize its universal quality, its personal appeal."

Much of what is contained in this volume comes from Ohiyesa's book, *The Soul of the Indian*. Other materials have come from his two autobiographical texts, *Indian Boyhood* and *From the Deep Woods to Civilization*. Still other material has come from *Old Indian Days, Indian Scout Talks: A Guide for Boy Scouts and Camp Fire Girls, The Indian Today: The Past and Future of the First Americans*, and a series of articles published in 1949 in *The New Bedford, Massachusetts Sunday Standard Times*, in which Ohiyesa's wife, Elaine Goodale Eastman, collated his thoughts on various subjects.

The reader who wishes to do a more scholarly analysis of Ohiyesa is encouraged to go back to these originals. It has been my intention to reveal the heart of the man and to let his spirit sing. I have tried to produce a book that is fair to Ohiyesa, appealing to the reader, and appropriate to our times.

If you, as a reader, have found yourself taken with the words of this most incisive and sensitive of Native American thinkers, I have done well.

Kent Nerburn
Bemidji, Minnesota 1993

About the Editor

Kent Nerburn, a Ph.D. in theology and art, is editor of *Native American Wisdom* and author of the highly acclaimed book, *Letters to My Son — Reflections on Becoming a Man*. He directed Project Preserve, an award-winning education program in oral history on the Red Lake Ojibwe Reservation, and has been involved in many facets of Indian education. He is a member of the National Indian Education Association and has served as consultant for curriculum development to the American Indian Institute in Norman, Oklahoma. He lives with his wife, Louise Mengelkoch, and family in Bemidji, Minnesota.

The Classic Wisdom Collection
of
New World Library

As You Think by James Allen. Edited and with an Introduction by Marc Allen.

Native American Wisdom. Compiled and with an Introduction by Kent Nerburn and Louise Mengelkoch.

The Art of True Healing by Israel Regardie. Edited and updated by Marc Allen.

Letters to a Young Poet by Rainer Maria Rilke. Translated by Joan M. Burnham with an Introduction by Marc Allen.

The Green Thoreau. Selected and with an Introduction by Carol Spenard LaRusso.

Political Tales & Truth of Mark Twain. Edited and with an Introduction by David Hodge and Stacey Freeman.

The Wisdom of Women. Selected and with an Introduction by Carol Spenard LaRusso.

The Soul of an Indian and Other Writings from Ohiyesa. Edited and with an Introduction by Kent Nerburn.